Rejoice In The Lord Always

Rejoice In The Lord Always

Anna Magdalene Handley

To order additional copies of this book, contact:
Xlibris Corporation
1-800-618-969
www.Xlibris.com.au
Orders@Xlibris.com.au
502234

Contents

The Beginning of my Christian Walk

Authors Notes

Recently I've become aware that God is the most important part of my life. There would be no life without Him.

He tells me to have faith that He can and will shoulder all my worries. He gives me strength to carry the burdens I must, while I wait for the inevitable blessings that come to those who wait.

May you all come to know His undying love and care for us. May you let Him help and guide you through your life. May you love Him back by loving His brethren.

Acknowledgements

Thank you and God bless all my support workers, family and friends past and present, who have inspired some of this poetry and lyrics. Especially through the tedious and tiresome hours of helping me edit these poems and pictures. I truly appreciate their care and consideration expressed for me. Particularly Janet Hayward, David Cubitt, Lara Stone, Debra Varlow, Eve Ward , Michael Visser, Peter Kemp, Owen, Tatenda-Ishe Sakatari, Petra Fischer, Michelle Guilding, Angela Meyer, Helen Denman, Kobi Bennett, Melissa Byers, Anne John, Luzviminda Arthur, Tracee Edwards, 1P0ierre Figuera, Lee Figuera, Sarah Handley, Lynden Young *and many more.*

Thankyou to all who have inspired Some of this poetry along this crazy journey especially Tatenda-Ishe Sakatari, Cindy Porteus, Steve and Chris Watson/brown, Megs Bennett, Mikey Cheetham, Dustan Bell, Lucas Connell, James Macpherson, Lindsey Clarke, My son Jesse, my brothers and sisters, Mum, and the loving memory of Dad and my bro Joey.

May you be always aware that God is truly here for us, no matter how things appear.

I particularly wish to express my undying gratitude and love to Jesus my Saviour who has encouraged and inspired me through thick and thin, I could not have printed this book without You.

Introducing some of my poetry to be explained through my autobiography to be published soon.

Go With The Flow

The world will go on spinning
As our children go on growing
We can't ask life to slow down
We can't ask life to wait for us to catch up
All we can do is flow along with it
As the mountain stream does
4th JUNE 1993

An Identity Crisis

I'm home! I'm home!

But that's not the end of the story

I'm home! I'm home! and depressingly devoid of glory

What was once glowing with intrigue

Holds no delights now

That free spirit is of the past

I hunger for what the body won't allow

Grieving is the first part of re-creating the self

So grieve it all out

For creation is coming without a doubt

Free Spirit

I spread my wings and fly
Feeling I can never die
Off we go to find visions of splendour
Where we could end up on a bender
In the haunting quietness
No moment can be relived
The moon and stars still shine on
Squatters and lovers alike
Even if we tell each other to take a hike
A health direction is forming
From shadows, healing is dawning

A Twinkle In The Eye

In the sweetest lovers' dance

Hearts are a-flutter with wild romance

Angels twinkle in their eyes

Heaven lies in their sighs

Thurs 31 Dec 1991—Sat 11 Jan 1992

Language Of The Soul

Let's speak the language of the soul

Look you deep into me

What sustains it all?

Smile, coz it's free

Laugh and fear cannot be

Sometimes words are codswallop

Sometimes power is of the spirit

Beyond these states of mind

Beneath these games that blind

Let's speak the language of the soul

Look you deep into me

What sustains it all?

Refreshing

Chorus

Like a breath of fresh air

You gave me your care

You wouldn't dare to

Hold love inside

You loved me for free

I didn't make you love me

Verse 1

We wouldn't let our bodies

Make us feel their constant pain

In bubbling spontaneity

Laughter was our game

We were on a mystery tour

Awaiting what became

Love in effervescence

Lit our hearts aflame

Chorus

On & On It Goes

I've been side tracked

Caught up in the fuzzy race of life

Where wild animals attack

One can blow ones stack

The hot tears can flow

And on and on it goes

Till our burdens threaten to crush

And the weeping blood does gush

Feeling my way in the dark

I saw in your heart a spark

Reminiscent of my purpose

But only I could bring me to surface

You gave me an inkling

To open up my soul

This is my song

Of the moment now gone

When immortal music bled long

Beauty, not right or wrong

Now I see

That through my soul it flows

And on and on it goes

Healing Unity

I don't want to be rich and famous
I just want to be healed
Can't you feel the healing unity?
That exists inside eternally
Across all barriers it's extending
Where any disharmony finds it's ending
Beneath all our dreams of our mortality
Our immortal soul is our reality

Each Brand New Day

When a man views earth's wonders

From some mountain height

He does not spend time

Dwelling on the faints & fights

That marks his upward journey

To drink in the sights

Breathe in the rich blessing

Of each brand new day

Forget what lies behind

Or what you've done on the way

Don't gather again

The burdens of past

For weal or woe

Each day is cast

Let The Child

Let the child within

Let the child within dance with rapture

Truly sacred is

Sacred is the moment of now

With things of wonder

With things of wonder to ponder

One Man's Trash

One man's trash
Is another man's treasure
One man's pain
Is another man's pleasure
A fossilized nappy
May be your future jewel
An open mind
Could be tomorrow's fuel

Wake Up!

Restore exquisite connection to the divine

Mere survival is not enough anymore

So immerse the weary soul till it sings

And let it overflow with a gentle power

Eternally unbreakable

No matter what happens

Hell Bent And Driven

When I awake from my trance
My obsession leads a merry dance
Of which my greedy soul loves to dine
Throwing chaos to the confines of time
Clinging to healing with grasping death grip
Leaves me wanting for a desperate sip
Born is true healing from inside to out
Be here this holy instant and remove all doubt
It is needless to search for what's already found
It's already here when I look around
Healed of obsession is what I seek
A freak becoming mild and meek

Shock Value

Travelled a trip through the red hot dust

In their old car they must trust

They two strode into this one horse town

Stretching the status quo of what goes down

A few cow-cockies held up the bar

Wondering at the audacity that could take these two far

An intriguing hairstyle with protruding incense sticks, alight

Scattering scented ashes, warding off any fights

Exuding an air of exiting danger

To any interfering stranger

In a loud and rasping voice

A thick rare steak was just her choice

She waved off the utensils

And hoped she wouldn't faint

As the bloody steak was slapped onto a plate

Blood dripped down and off her chin

And she just let it run.

The shock value is done

Get Real

To expose true threads of gold

Keep being true, watch it all unfold

Get real, get real

It's your end of the deal

Be not hasty

Life is tasty

Take time to savour

It's delicious flavour

Get out of your mind

Reality is more than our eyes can find

Underneath all appearances

Ultimate reality glitters in the dark

Get real, get real

It's your end of the deal

You Ain't Lost Nothin'

Your safety left
Coz I walked out the door
When I came back home
I wasn't the same anymore
Different hair
Different voice
Different body
With the same heart
It's what inside that counts
Here right from the start
You ain't lost nothin' my baby
No you ain't lost nothin'

Genuine Spark

Caught your genuine spark
It radiates from you
The kind that you can't hide
No doubt contagious too
So if I beat my chest
And dance on tabletop
Just know I caught your spark
Oh I don't wanna stop
Deep in our heart of heart of hearts
We all got that genuine spark
The kind that dances and renews
Lights a dying fuse
It spreads delicious threads
Till all our souls feel wed
Pulsing electricity
I'll strike you if you strike me

Tangled Up In Tango

Tangled up in tango

With my wheelchair and commode

I will not let my pride

Steal the healing peace of mind

What frees me from limits?

Is where healing peace I find

Let go the limits

And discover this passionate tango

Dynamics of a woman

I am a woman

I am a mother

I move

I sing

I give

I love

I live

The Narrow Black Door

In the city, on the sidewalk

Is a door that's narrow and black

Out steps an enchanting young fellow

Who graciously invites me back

Through the door I follow him

Trusting the goodness of his heart

A sweet melody plays from a well-loved piano

A saxophone lets out a sexy fart

As radiating fire draws me to the hearth

To sit upon the velvety rug

Dwelling in wonder on life's path

Seductively beckons harp string

Gentle strumming spreads sacred sound

Exuding charms bewitching

Where exquisite melody is found

As You Do

Hit and miss the target when you smack your son over your wheelchair

lap till you both crack up

As you do

Flipping over onto one's back, like a turtle when you're wheelchair bound

Using the opportunity to meditate

As you do

Not allowing the pee to thieve the peace just because it spilt on the floor

No good crying over spilt pee

As you do

Cut loose from what you 'should' do

As you do

Bopping deep down inside, when your just rollin' along

As you do

Talking crazy talk, and walking crazy walk

As you do

Laughing till you ache, seems like your gonna break

As you do

Risking all for adventure, and delighting in life's taste

As you do

Debating so intensely that you fall off your chair

As you do

Waxing off your wildly hairy face so it's not such a disgrace

As you do

Baby Let It Go

We're born perfect

Till we defect

That we can feel that pull

Of imagined obsession

Compulsive aggression

We put ourselves through so much pain

Till we realize we don't have to do it again

Hungry? Baby let it go

Grasping? Baby let life flow

It's wonderful to accept this journey

Without being addicted to the result

When we're frustrated or mad

Fearful or sad

We aren't being real

Which is our part of the deal

Forgotten? Baby let it go

Deluded? Baby let life flow

Comedy Striptease

Show a little skin

Pout that sexy thing

Sensual and erotic

High without narcotic

Twisting and turning

And Chinese burning

Can you please take off my shoe?

Which my muscles don't wanna do

This dance may seem like kama sutra

But it's really striptease ooh la, la

Move that naked heat

To that naked beat

But take special care

Not to rock and roll out of your chair

Wisdom Of Peace

The wisdom of peace
Brews like a stew
In life like the pot
Holding me, holding you
Taste this recipe once and
It's never forgot
It's not fattening
So you can eat up the lot

Unpredictable

Wisdom comes

On angel wings

Gentle whispers

In my heart I hear

Plan, dream

But don't expect

Unpredictable as the sea

One twist of fate

Then we shall see

The Sweetness You Can Taste

My heart is held in sweetest melody

Where it pulses and radiates its rays

Under stars, by the fire

The click-ity clack of trains jam along

With her sassy voice

Laying atop of a bed of his vibrating strings

There's a cloud of etheric bodies

Levitating slowly

Shed a tear

At the sweeteness you can taste

Luminous Eyes

Please stare into me

With your luminous eyes

There's something here

That I do recognize

Its like a tree

It is wondrous wise

It's how we all wanna be

Free from all disguise

Glad you didn't move away

Stick around with us man

And pluck guitar

In your 'veggie' van

Sing songs that tell us

How It's Not A Scam

Without you we'll all be broke

Coz you're a beaut bloke

Let's laugh until we choke

Cutt'n sick on our own joke

You

Okay leave your kissable lips here

For me to kiss

And leave your warm and slender body here

For me to hold

And please don't take your mind

I love how it opens

To synchronize with mine

Lifes Intricate Plan

All has my permission to happen

Who are we to complain

About life's intricate pattern

Or interfere with its pain

When mould grows and bubbles

It's just telling you

Look you don't have to eat this

I AM

Home

We can see the obstacles of life

As stones on which to stub our toes

Or as stepping-stones to take us home

Home to our strong, gentle heart of honor

Of chi, of life force energy to pour

Into the ordinariness

Where innately we know that

Beautiful things grow from poo

Rise Up In Song

What's the point

And why try

Try to run free from my jail

There are so many reasons

To rise up in song

For the growth of spirit

In reaching for the stars

For those who love

And encourage me to go so far

To illustrate

The power of spirit

To take me there

If I can do it

Then so can you

So I'll carry on

And rise up in song

Trees

Learn from a tree
To simply "be"
They speak to us
We may listen in a different way
Listen through the silence
Feel them speaking to your heart

Metamorphosis

Through my pain wracked desperate cries
Undoubtedly I metamorphosize
My true self
Steps forth from shadow
Into light
A slow motion shape changer
Learning not to fight

Essence

Droplets of dew drip from
Tendrils of vine
Ladybird hides in shade
Is it a sign?
That the world is changing
And rearranging
Still succulence is
Alchemised into wine
Delicious is every drip
Is it a crime?
Taste this elixir
Vital and sweet
Of love in its essence
Oh what a treat

Obi

Got them "wanna go to the beach too" blues

Just staring at the wall

It's the only place I've ever been before

But nobody takes me there no more

They leave me home with the lifeless ball

But that ball don't breathe it don't laugh or run

It just don't know how to have any fun

Gotta get there all by myself somehow

Maybe I'll hotwire a car

Maybe I'll be picked up by the law

Maybe I'll hitch a ride with the hound next-door

Maybe I'll be cooked and served up with coleslaw

Long Lost Twin

Hey Sista

Let's chuck a left here

Sprawl out on the grass

Read to each other

Lets pick a bunch of wild flowers

And stick them in our hair

What others think of us we don't care

I celebrate your victory

With a laugh a squeal and a shout

When you drop food all over the kitchen floor

And clean up without spinning out

I Lost My Voice

I lost my voice

On a sterilized wall

But I found it again

In Carnegie hall

I lost my jive

In a fast red fox

But I found it in my soul

On a gentle giants box

I lost my style

In a futile lonely rave

But I found it

When I tuned in

To the certain clear wave

Time Is Money

Time is money and I don't wanna know

We get all this stuff

That we just gotta maintain

It's a vicious cycle

That can drive you insane

Embarrassed and ashamed

Of taxing your time

I'm no accountant

I'm not interested in keeping

A policeman's eye on my time

I heal as I sing

As the music round me rings

Love Unstoppable

You may have been hurt by others

But this is me that's loving you now

Love ain't heavy honey

We can be afraid of love

Because we may not love ourselves

Then we fall into heavy traps of expectation

Love and fear cannot co-exist

Nothing can stop love

If I told you I love you I love you forever

Let ecstasy heal us to the tips of our fingers and toes

You may not want to admit it but

You've been loving me all along

You don't have to tell me . . . I feel it

Nothing Happens By Accident

It's all perfect
Life is no accident
The smiles, the affection, childhoods apple tart
The tears and deception, the falling apart
The love, the devotion, meeting hearts that dance
Letting fear come steal our peace while in trance
The flames of torment, bleeding with pain
The clearing of the slate and the starting again

The Vicious Cycle

We think we've gotta keep our chin up & be tough

Sometimes we must accept the help that comes our way

Don't bite the hand that feeds

You may not get it so good one day

Oh but she'll be right mate

Let's just sweep it all under the grate

And get on with the bbq

When the pressures of life

Press us down

The hardest thing is to be in it but not of it

And at the same time it's so simple

To just change your mind

The least impact we can have

Is to sit in a corner and do nothing

But if we do we'll probably be taken to the loony bin

Why do we think we have the right

To kill everything else to live?

And why do we now make ourselves live longer

So we can kill the world for a little longer

It's a vicious cycle

But, anything is possible

Let's begin viciously cycling out this vicious cycle

Once you begin help will come

Life Is For The Sharing

We are all in the same boat

No one is more "special" than anyone else

We are the human family

When we're over the moon about something

It's natural to share it

It makes me feel as if you're ashamed of me

If you don't

Maybe you're ashamed of yourself

Let's heal

Let's share

Are you ready?

Real Life

Whatever we physically do

Is of no relevance in life

It all means peanuts in the end

The ego places a lot of importance on relationships, livelihood, diet,

physical appearance, what makes a healthy lifestyle, doing the right thing,

sex

And some of these things are good but we needn't make

Anything into our gods to control us

Cause we mean much more than that

We have a destiny

We are all the love in the universe

So what would love do now?

The Great Parachute

Time, it is intangible
Times have been unforgettable
You're part of my life forever now
Becoming estranged I won't allow
In life may you always follow your dreams
May you jump into life with lots of whoops and screams
May your ride through life be gentle like a great parachute
May you learn from where you go and what you refute
May you develop the love that resides in your soul
And learn that by giving it away, love always unfolds

Dear Brother

Ever since you were a child

I've appreciated your smile

And your nonsensical sense of humour

That reminds me of Puma's in bloomers at Montezumas

Now that we are adults your perseverance is impressive

Your non-conforming ways are progressive

I hope to see into your spirited heart

Where there lives a work of art

The G. P.

We're off to see the gypsum practitioner

To be plastered up at the gym

To relieve our cruel disorders

And be renewed from tip to toe

Softly I hear whispers that it's all just been a con

All a con for money not for love or beauty or song

And they don't care if you live or die

My G.P. says with a big cheesy grin

Any disease is dead when brought to the gym

You don't have to know how bad it is

Just get better cause you've got lots of life to live

Blessed Frustration

Sometimes there's just no way to hold back the frustration

Like the volcano

Coz life's a bitch when I feel so helpless

I love it when you admire my fire

Sometimes people take it personal

Instead of helping it out of me

Blessed frustration is pushing me to get free

Isn't caring a friend's job

Am I paying you to be my friend?

It's so easy to smudge the lines

Sometimes there's no way to hold back the tears

Like the tide

If you are gentle with me I'll be gentle with you

We might break

Last night I fell out of bed again

I was not gonna get the ambo's this time

And I got back into the bed

Where there's a will there's a way

Defining Oneself

I am defining myself
Sex makes me fall in love
Caught between the devil & the deep blue sea
Like so many other things in this world
One is momentary
And the other endures forever
So let's not go there
Coz what endures forever
Is more important
And it's all backwards
Like so many other things
In this crazy world

Kick The Bucket

Kick the bucket with gusto

Pass on over in style

Go to meet your maker

But you can't even take your smile

You'll be pushing up the daisies

Man like crazy

You'll haunt us and you'll taunt us

And your signs will let us know

It's never too late

To contemplate

When you got to go

You got to go

Death Or Fate

Can't give up now
I've come so far
Your smile encourages me
To go there
We can be sucked in by the illusion
Coz life's full of challenges
When do we get a break?
For what do we wait?
For death or fate?
Thanks that I'm never really alone
It's never too late
To bless it all
For teaching us
That our holiness is our salvation

This Life Is For Something Else

Let's make it all better

Better late than never

Let's make it all better

And let the music heal and soothe us

It calls us

When we're ready we come

To forgive, heal

And watch the unfolding

None has all the answers

There's more than what we see

It's contagious

It's spreading

It's medicine

It's what we need

Tommy
(Written to my Dad)

VERSE ONE

We're all equal in death

Ya gotta go when ya gotta go

Take the time to reflect

On with the show, on with the show

CHORUS

Oh Tommy, tenacity's a gift you gave me

Oh Tommy now your spirit's free

Oh Tommy walk with God real far

Oh Tommy coz you're a good kid and we love ya x 2

VERSE TWO

Just returning the favour

Funny how the tables turn

Of your life's sweet flavour

Much to learn, much to learn

CHORUS

And we love ya x 4

Forever Strong
(For Mum)

All is well
Is what you say
It picks us up
When we have a bad day

What you give
Is a heartfelt song
Forever strong
Even if we're wrong

Life is interesting
Its music and truth
You are interested in everything
From the garden to youth

You are a gift to me
Your music sets me free
You remind me that God gives me His power
To carry through every hour

You're doing a good job
If kids used to make you mad
You teach me to meet my challenges
And see the good in the bad

The Beginning
of my
Christian Walk

Living Water

I am Your child

You are my Daddy

You have been waiting a long time

For me to let You into my heart

And receive Your love which You offer free

Only a long time for me

Just a breath for You

Your perfect love casts out my fear

I am overflowing with Your love

So that I don't mind giving You my life

You are my power, oh how I have missed You

And I want to be with You through the broken places of life

Only You can fill me with living water

The Miraculous Words (To My Son)

The most precious gift

I can give you

Are the miraculous words:

Life is up to you

God gave us all free will

Your heavenly Daddy waits for your welcome

To bless every moment

So they can all be sacred

When you are sad, mad or generally feel bad

You can be sure

That with God, anything is possible

If you step out of your comfort zone

God promises that empowerment will come

If you ask for His help

Jesus the Risk Taker

Mostly we think of Jesus

As gentle, loving and kind

But when Jesus was on earth

He had to be a wild risk taker

He took a risk

To preach the Word

About the saving grace of God

In the most hostile of times and places

He took a risk to die

For His people who cursed Him

Risking His plan to be rejected

He didn't let fear stop him

From Loving others

Don't let fear stop you

If Jesus was a risk taker

Would you also take a risk for love?

Patience

When times are tough
Be patient
There is obviously
Something good coming
That is why
You are still here
To support me
After seeing my screaming
And tears of frustration
Good is coming

Healing of the Heart

Excitement mounts

As anything is possible

As my heart heals so will my body

I am learning to rely on God

This is so beautiful I don't want to get better

But as God is my author

He is promising that things will be even brighter

As He always has our very best in mind for us

Thank God For You
(To Tatenda)

Thank God for you, mudiwa

And for the awesome gift you've given me

It's worth much more than gold

This kind of intimate friend that comes for free

But mere gold is too inadequate

To pay for my eternal life

To love on through my suffering

and hold on through my strife

I treasure this certificate

You've put into my heart

It reveals to me, the blessed plan

To fellowship with our Creator again

Eternal Power

The kind of healing
I have under my belt
Will always minister to me
For as long as I need
When the time is right
My body will be restored
But it's not so important anymore
I have the Power
Eternally on my side
To help me remain peaceful, loving and kind
No matter what happens
I am already free from Fred
anxiety and disappointment
This is the kind of Love
That I have always wanted

You are Faithful

Every moment
Of every day
Is full of reasons
That make me see
How faithful You are
Keep coming
And making
Your presence felt
As You are faithful
Forever

Deepening

The law is of the heart now
We can push You away easy
By our anger, resentment and fear
When we get impatient
When we tell a lie
Even a little white lie
Then we find
That You are not near
We cannot feel Your presence
Like a delicate perfume
That spreads across the world
Bringing out, our loving kindness
But if we don't obey
We shut ourselves out

Miracle

Bless life's miraculous trials
They make it sacred
Without life's miraculous trials
I would not be here
To gain the precious gifts
Of courage and patience
While waiting for a miracle
I realise I need merely
To claim Your miraculous healing
You will burst into my life
I am patiently waiting
For You to wreck me
With Your love
Please come . . .

Life Through Baptism

We are renewed and invigorated through

The wonderful plan of "The Most High"

Who sent an aspect of Himself to heal His creation

He would perform an act of astounding love

So our hearts would melt

We can run into His arms and be loved for eternity

As we are His precious treasures

Restoration

Oh my eternal heavenly Father

Thank you for Your love and care over me

Being my medicine in all situations

For restoring my soul and body

Fill me with Your goodness

So I can be served

To all the world to be Your light

God Is Just

There was a girl
Who'd done some horrific stuff
She asks if God will punish her
Her pastor is torn between
Revealing God's love or God's justice
But then he remembers
That all sin is already punished
In our sweet Jesus
Life has a way of punishing us
For whatever we do to others
We are so grateful
That God is just

God Is Mercy

Everything that God is

We are not

God can forgive

The most evil sins

But we can remember

God is mercy at His heart

Through His mercy

God comes as the dayspring

From on high to visit us

Using our human mortality

He has shown us that we can live life to the full

Only if we have Him in our hearts

I Stand Convicted

For my unfaithful lack of trust

No matter how impossible my life may seem

God can make it so sweet

We are all called to Him again

He who is seeking His children

In the dark night of our soul

He invites us to transparency

To be the saints He has named us

My Hearts Desire

God's fire burns deep within me

Igniting me with passion to be free

With sparkling eyes and feisty cries

Certain will I stay

Persistent, consistent, insistent, determined

That I am whole today

Can't be free if I try

Until my gut is busting

Because now I remember

That struggle is a result

Of trying instead of trusting

I trust God to direct my hearts desire

And of this I shall never tire

Never tire of His burning desire

To love on me for free

As through the puzzles of life I forage

My heart's desire is to have the courage

To abide in Him

Bless God

I am so moved

By Gods overflowing love for me

That I will honour Him and bless Him back

In His word Jesus says

If you give a cup of cold water

To one of the least of my brethren

You give it to me

So we can bless him

By loving everyone

No matter the reception

Everyone is precious

No one is not worth my lavish love

The Unstoppable Christ

Jesus, You are our role model

Of life renewed

Awesome are you Jesus

You who beat death

Hallelujah! Forever we will praise your name

For You and the Father are one

We will exhault your mighty name

Thank you for your exceedingly glorious gifts

Gifts that we can share

I Can Bless

All discouraging is dead in me now

No more complaining, criticising or condemnation

I can bless by being encouraging

Only through the power

Of the Holy Spirit

Can I bless

Whoever comes in my door

To care for me

Taming The Tongue

God's word says
A lot of our problems are fixed
If we follow His way
If we don't speak
It keeps us gentle and meek
And we avoid a lot of unnecessary pain
When we don't play that game

Blessings For Joe, My Bro

Oh rascally rapscallion

Have some cheek

And have a trance

Remember 'boo not be afrab coz now He's wiff you'

Oh gentle one, when you were gentle

Thanks for your acceptance

And your kindly love and care for me

Though you scared me at times

Farewell fellow soldier fighting for life

Now we're one short, we'll miss you

The Blessing

God's word says

His son was wounded

So we might be healed

He died

So that we might have life

He was made sin

So that we might be righteous

He was rejected

So that we might be accepted

He was made a curse

So that we might enter into the blessing

So God is so awesome

For His gift of His son

To us

And that now we can move

From the curse

Into the blessing